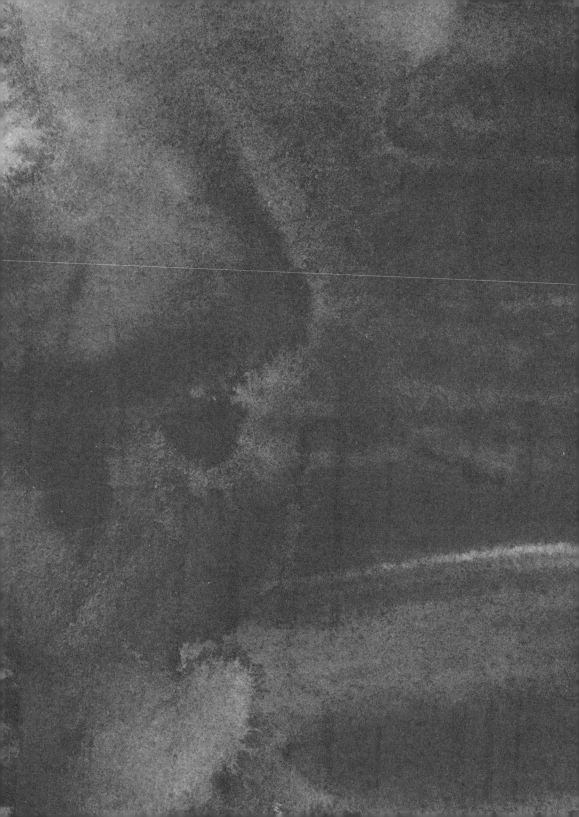

Made to Flourish

MADE TO

Flourish

Cultivating an Abundant Life

BETH MOORE

TYNDALE
MOMENTUM

The Tyndale nonfiction imprint

Visit Tyndale online at tyndale.com.

Visit Tyndale Momentum online at tyndalemomentum.com.

Visit Beth Moore online at lproof.org.

TYNDALE, Tyndale's quill logo, *Tyndale Momentum*, and the Tyndale Momentum logo are registered trademarks of Tyndale House Publishers. Tyndale Momentum is the nonfiction imprint of Tyndale House Publishers, Carol Stream, Illinois.

Made to Flourish: Cultivating an Abundant Life

Designed by Julie Chen

Edited by Stephanie Rische

Published in association with Yates & Yates, LLP (www.yates2.com).

ISBN 978-1-4964-4096-9

Printed in China

26	25	24	23	22	21	20
7	6	5	4	3	2	1

Contents

Introduction

I have been enamored with Christ's teaching on the vine and the branches since I cut my teeth on Bible study, and I've taught about His call to fruitfulness as an essential part of life's satisfaction for at least twenty years. The spectacular thing about Scripture, however, is that, like no other book held in human hands, its ink may be dry but it is the furthest thing from dead. The words are alive and active, and the Holy Spirit who inspired them can animate the most familiar passage and spring it to fresh life again in your soul.

It happened to me in Tuscany a year ago, on a dream trip I took with my daughters. The place was otherworldly. We stayed three nights at an inn on a hillside in the upper quadrant of a vineyard. I could stand on the grounds and in every direction I looked, I saw vines.

On our way into town by taxi one morning, we saw the last of the harvesters walking the rows—inspecting the vines and clipping the final heavy clusters of fruit. Captivated, I felt like I was watching live reenactments of some of Christ's own parables. It was not lost on me that one of His final exhortations to His disciples was, essentially, "Be immensely fruitful" (John 15:5-8). The image of the vineyard has consumed me ever since.

When Jesus told His disciples, "My Father is the gardener" (John 15:1, NLT), He wasn't using random imagery to sketch His point. From the very first book in the Bible, we discover that God is a gardener:

The LORD God planted a garden.
GENESIS 2:8

From the beginning, it's God Himself with hoe and spade. It's God who's afoot with herbs and bulbs. It's God with the knack and no *Farmers' Almanac*.

It's a wonder to me that God would choose to slowly grow what He could have simply created grown. Why on earth would He go to the trouble to plant a garden forced to sprout rather than commanding it into existence, full bloom? Why leave His desk and get His pant legs soiled?

Because God likes watching things grow.

This metaphor plays out throughout Scripture as He tends His people with care, skill, and intention. When Jesus began His ministry on earth, He took this idea to a whole new level, revealing that He Himself is the Vine. He invites us to the sacred ground of abiding, calling us to flourish in the abundant life He offers.

In the following pages, I invite you to explore the fruitful life through the language of the garden—and the words of the Master Gardener Himself.

Beth Moore

Horticulture

hor·ti·cul·ture

[ˈhȯr-tə-ˌkəl-chər] NOUN

1. the science and art of growing fruits, vegetables, flowers, or ornamental plants

*T*he Bible uses gardening terms for the acts of God time and again. In 2 Samuel 7:10, God is described as appointing a people and not placing them, but rather planting them where He wanted them. Psalm 94:9 says God planted the ear on man, and according to Luke 22:51, Jesus could also clearly replant one, should that be necessary. Words like *rooted* and *uprooted* and *grounded* all speak the language of horticulture. God is the master gardener, and we, His tender seeds.

The Lord has chosen you and planted you, and He is preparing you for a great harvest. He's getting you ready to thrive and flourish and bear much fruit. If we submit ourselves to His ways, mysterious and painful though they may be at times, we will find that it's all part of the process that enables us to grow and bear fruit.

The LORD God planted a garden in Eden, in the east,

and there he put the man whom he had formed.

And out of the ground the LORD God made to spring up

every tree that is pleasant to the sight and good for food.

GENESIS 2:8-9

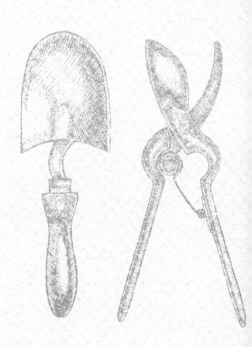

GOD DELIGHTS
IN WATCHING
THINGS GROW.

Dirt

dirt

['dərt] NOUN
1. loose or packed soil
or sand; earth

*C*reation brought out the earthy side of heaven. On the third day, God created dirt and liked it. It is a poor soul who confuses dirt with filth or soil with soiled.

Dirt drapes this spinning rock we call earth with a fine epidermis—pocked, porous, and thirsty. Dirt accommodates ants with both heap and hole. It memorializes every creature afoot, lizard and leopard alike, with at least a fleeting footprint. The dirt under an elephant's toenails may end up as sunscreen for his delicate hide when he tosses it by trunk onto his back.

The fact is, in the hands of the consummate Potter, dirt is fodder for His wheel.

After bringing the universe into being by nothing but His voice, God thrust His hands downward into the soil (*adamah* in Hebrew) and fashioned a human (*adam*).

The English word *human* literally means "a creature of earth," from the word *humus*, or ground.[1]

The idea of God at arm's length is a comfortable thought. We could imagine the Creator with arms long enough to keep His face from getting dusty through the whole creative ordeal, but blowing breath into the human's nostrils sketches a different posture.

Here we have a Maker leaning low, near to the ground. Here we have God who is high and lifted up but is now bending over, animating dust. God, mouth-to-nose with man.

The LORD God formed the man of dust from the ground

and breathed into his nostrils the breath of life,

and the man became a living creature.

GENESIS 2:7

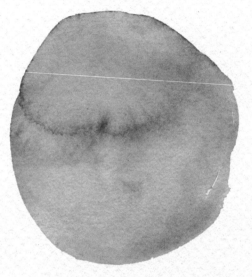

GOD CREATED DIRT
AND LIKED IT.

Clusters

17

clus·ter

[ˈklə-stər] NOUN

1. a number of similar things
that occur together

$\mathcal{G}$rapes don't grow solo; they only grow in clusters. Scale the world's finest hills and forge her fertile valleys, and you'll find her clusters in all sorts of colors—pink, purple, crimson, green, black, dark blue, yellow, and orange—up to a mind-boggling ten thousand varieties.

The Hebrew word for "cluster" is *eshcol*. When the Israelite spies surveyed the Promised Land, one branch with a single cluster of grapes had to be carried by two grown men on a pole between them—that's some kind of heavy fruit. One horticulturist suggests these grapes were of the Syrian variety known for producing clusters of between twenty and thirty pounds.[2]

Thousands of years later, in that same land, a Vine grew, which from all outward appearances was common. The Vine made a promise to a dozen branches, if only they'd abide.

Much fruit. Heavy fruit. Weighty fruit. The most profitable fruit in all the world.

Through Jesus Christ, you are in the bloodline of the Bible's ancient fruit bearers. Together with the rest of your divinely called cluster, you are called to bear much fruit. Heavy fruit. Weighty fruit. The most profitable fruit in all the world.

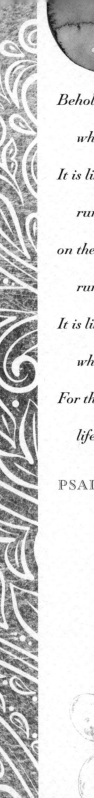

Behold, how good and pleasant it is

when brothers dwell in unity!

It is like the precious oil on the head,

running down on the beard,

on the beard of Aaron,

running down on the collar of his robes!

It is like the dew of Hermon,

which falls on the mountains of Zion!

For there the LORD has commanded the blessing,

life forevermore.

PSALM 133

THIS IS
THE BLESSING:
LIFE
FOREVERMORE.

Vinedresser

vine·dress·er

[ˈvīn-ˌdre-sər] NOUN

1. a person who cultivates
and prunes grapevines

*W*hen Jesus told the parable of the fig tree midway through Luke's Gospel, He turned up the volume on the vinedresser's patience and compassion. He earnestly desired to delay judgment so he could work with the tree and urge it to fruitfulness. If, after the determined length of time, the tree still didn't produce anything, he'd agree to the brisk swing of an ax.

Don't dream that the Vinedresser won't dig around in your well-manicured soil. He doesn't even mind tearing up your landscaping, if that's what it takes.

And He won't just go digging up your old skeletons and unearth a few fossils of your family tree. He's liable to dig up all sorts of things that got buried alive.

But if He does, you need not wonder why. The Vinedresser digs around the roots of a tree to stimulate fruit, to prod and goad that plant into productivity, to shock it a bit with a shovel so it will wake up and do what it's meant to do.

This is the grace of God. This is the transforming power of the Cross. This is the way of the God of countless chances.

Let me sing for my beloved

my love song concerning his vineyard:

My beloved had a vineyard

on a very fertile hill. . . .

What more was there to do for

my vineyard,

that I have not done in it?

ISAIAH 5:1, 4

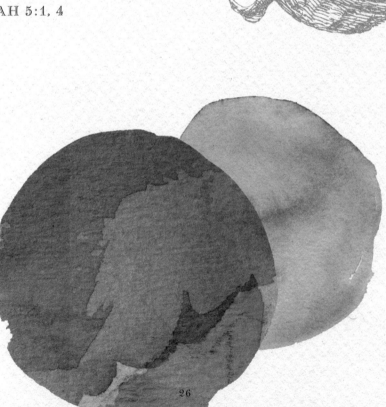

THE
VINEDRESSER
ISN'T AFRAID TO
GET A LITTLE DIRT
UNDER HIS
FINGERNAILS.

Terroir

ter·roir

[ˌterˈwär] NOUN
1. the combination of
factors including soil,
climate, and sunlight
that gives wine grapes
their distinctive
character

*O*ne of the loveliest terms in viticulture is *terroir*, meaning "sense of place."[3] You can see its relationship to the word *terre*, meaning "earth," but terroir encompasses more than ground. It captures the interplay between factors such as soil, climate, the plant itself, and its orientation toward the sun. Together, these factors ultimately shape the "personality" of the resulting fruit.[4]

We are not so different from those vines that need a conducive environment to grow in. We spend our lives looking for home. We crave a sense of place. We are roots dangling in the air, carried by the wind, looking frantically for fitting terroir. But that's part of the mystery. Part of the romance, really. For here and now, our terroir cannot be found in any plot of terrestrial ground.

As followers of Christ, our primary terroir, or "sense of place," is Christ. Jesus is our singular place of abiding, the terroir of every true branch. The former vine, Israel, was rooted in the land, but Jesus didn't call His disciples to cling to the land. He called them to cling to Him, even as they went to the far-flung corners of the earth.

I am the true vine, and my Father is the vinedresser. . . .

Whoever abides in me and I in him,

he it is that bears much fruit,

for apart from me you can do nothing.

JOHN 15:1, 5

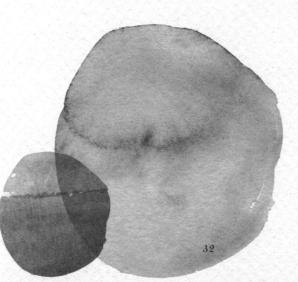

WE ALL CRAVE
A SENSE OF
PLACE.

Altitude

al·ti·tude

[ˈal-tə-ˌtüd] NOUN
1. the vertical elevation of
an object above a surface
(such as sea level or land)
of a planet or natural
satellite

*W*ithout valleys, there are no hills. You can't recognize hill country without low country. You can't adequately revere a rise without respecting the risk of a fall. In Scripture, hills and mountains are not just about altitudes. They're about action. Movement. Ups and downs. They're about ascending and descending, like angels on Jacob's ladder.

Hills require intentionality. You can't just casually walk them. You have to climb them. You engage your calves and thighs, and your legs will remind you days later that you did. You have to watch your footing on the slopes, or you'll slip.

But once you make it to the top, the panorama is your prize. For anyone with any sense, altitude changes attitude. Up there, you get a whole different perspective on where you've been and where you're going.

In the wilderness prepare the way of the LORD;

 make straight in the desert a highway for our God.

Every valley shall be lifted up,

 and every mountain and hill be made low;

the uneven ground shall become level,

 and the rough places a plain.

And the glory of the LORD shall be revealed,

 and all flesh shall see it together,

 for the mouth of the LORD has spoken.

ISAIAH 40:3-5

ALTITUDE
CHANGES
ATTITUDE.

Nature

na·ture

[ˈnā-chər] NOUN
1. the inherent character
or basic constitution of a
person or thing; essence

$\mathcal{N}$othing is natural about planting your roots in the soil of the resolute knowledge that you are personally, immeasurably, and immutably loved by God. It's not normal to believe any such thing. It's certainly not normal for this to be the belief you hold deepest of all. Such a belief is divine. It's muscular. It's protein, not carbohydrate. It requires "strength to comprehend . . . the breadth and length and height and depth, and to know the love of Christ that surpasses knowledge" (Ephesians 3:18-19). What if we sought the pure strength to comprehend how inconceivably loved we are? What if we sought that love like the marvel it really is?

There is only one love that cannot let go. There is only one love that refuses to ebb and flow despite the conditions.

Neither death nor life, nor angels nor rulers, nor things present nor things to come, nor powers, nor height nor depth, nor anything else in all creation, will be able to separate us from the love of God in Christ Jesus our Lord.

ROMANS 8:38-39

THERE IS
ONLY ONE LOVE
THAT CANNOT
LET GO.

Alfresco

al·fres·co

[al-ˈfre-(ˌ)skō]
ADJECTIVE or ADVERB
1. taking place or located
in the open air; outdoors

*M*ost of Jesus' parables send us out of the house and into the elements. When we're outside, exposed to the elements, we're reminded how little we really do control. We're hit afresh with the revelation that we're not as self-reliant as we thought we were. It's at once downsizing and upsizing. We can sense our smallness and God's vastness.

It's not that we can handle our challenges indoors; it's that it's easier to believe our illusions of control. It's also easier to adapt to artificial light. Out in the wild, where we feel our smallest, our significance doesn't shrink. It swells. It is this very God who looks the world over to strengthen hearts committed to Him. It is this very God who plants roots in fields, not floors.

What I'm trying to say is that grapevines don't grow well in terrariums.

The heavens proclaim the glory of God.

The skies display his craftsmanship.

Day after day they continue to speak;

night after night they make him known.

They speak without a sound or word;

their voice is never heard.

Yet their message has gone throughout the earth,

and their words to all the world.

PSALM 19:1-4, NLT

REAL BEAUTY
IS FOUND
UNDER THE
SAME SKY AS
VULNERABILITY.

Symbiosis

sym·bi·o·sis

[sim-bē- ō-səs] NOUN
1. the living together in
more or less intimate
association or close union
of two dissimilar organisms

*Y*ou are a planting of the Lord, and your soil is a blend of elements He is using to grow you in symbiotic cooperation with the absolute necessities of sun and rain. All sorts of conditions are being orchestrated over your head and under your feet to enhance your growth . . . and much of it is beyond the vision of your naked eye.

Christ will make his home in your hearts as you trust in him. Your roots will grow down into God's love and keep you strong. And may you have the power to understand, as all God's people should, how wide, how long, how high, and how deep his love is. May you experience the love of Christ, though it is too great to understand fully. Then you will be made complete with all the fullness of life and power that comes from God.

Now all glory to God, who is able, through his mighty power at work within us, to accomplish infinitely more than we might ask or think.

EPHESIANS 3:17-20, NLT

YOU ARE
A PLANTING
OF THE LORD.

Roots

root

['rüt] NOUN
1. the usually underground
part of a seed plant body

*D*own is the way up with God. There's no bearing fruit upward without first taking root downward. There are no shortcuts. No special dispensations. No exceptions for exceptional people. No special entitlements. Oh, it may seem so for a while, but a shallowly rooted plant won't pass the test of time.

In the parable of the sower, Jesus describes what happens when plants don't take root. People can respond to His words with open arms and ecstatic joy, but if they don't take root, they will fall away.

The shoot can't last without the root.

The seed is the word of God. The ones along the path are those who have heard; then the devil comes and takes away the word from their hearts, so that they may not believe and be saved. And the ones on the rock are those who, when they hear the word, receive it with joy. But these have no root; they believe for a while, and in time of testing fall away. And as for what fell among the thorns, they are those who hear, but as they go on their way they are choked by the cares and riches and pleasures of life, and their fruit does not mature. As for that in the good soil, they are those who, hearing the word, hold it fast in an honest and good heart, and bear fruit with patience.

LUKE 8:11-15

DOWN
IS THE
WAY UP
WITH GOD.

Humus

hu·mus

[ˈhyü-məs] NOUN
1. a brown or black
complex variable material
resulting from partial
decomposition of plant or
animal matter and forming
the organic portion of soil

I don't know what your soil looks like at this point in your life, but I'm going to guess that, unless you're among the rarest exceptions, something terrible has happened to you at one point or another.

Tossed right alongside the teeming life in your soil, death resides—ready, humble, and willing to enrich and increase all that lives. All sorts of deaths become humus in the ground of the human experience. This may mean the death of some dreams. The death of some hopes. The death of plans. The death of certain relationships.

Here's the big reveal: it didn't kill you. It didn't kill me, either. I thought it would. I bet you did too. But here we are, you and me, very much alive. Whether we wanted to be or not.

We're plantings of the Lord, in cylinders of soil already plenty fertile. The remaining question—and no small one, at that—is not whether we have what it takes to be extraordinarily fruitful but whether we're willing to expose our tender roots to the odd concoction of life and death that makes us grow.

"As he sowed, some fell along the path and was trampled underfoot,

and the birds of the air devoured it. And some fell on the rock,

and as it grew up, it withered away, because it had no moisture.

And some fell among thorns, and the thorns grew up with it

and choked it. And some fell into good soil and grew and

yielded a hundredfold." As he said these things, he called out,

"He who has ears to hear, let him hear."

LUKE 8:5-8

ARE YOU
WILLING TO EXPOSE
YOUR TENDER ROOTS
TO THE ODD CONCOCTION
OF LIFE AND DEATH
THAT MAKES US
GROW?

Rhizosphere

rhi·zo·sphere

[ˈrī-zə-ˌsfir] NOUN

1. soil that surrounds
and is influenced by
the roots of a plant

*T*he most vital underground element for any plant is called the rhizosphere, "the cylinder of soil surrounding each plant root."[5] In the words of my friend Farmer Fred, it's "where the real life takes place. The rhizosphere is the interface where the root touches the soil. Where that interface connects is where all the life happens."

For the sake of our present metaphor, you, a planting of the Lord, have your own rhizosphere. You are rooted in a cylinder of soil, and for that soil to be good and fertile ground where you can flourish, it must be a mass of all manner of organic matter: bacteria, algae, fungi, yeasts, protozoa, bugs, earthworms, and the like.

Imagine it. If you are planted in really rich soil, that means one little teaspoon holds millions of microbes. It also produces ample evidence of both life and death. In other words, all of it matters. Even unwanted endings. Even crushing losses. Even death itself.

I am sure that neither death nor life,

nor angels nor rulers,

nor things present nor things to come, nor powers,

nor height nor depth, nor anything else in all creation,

will be able to separate us from

the love of God in Christ Jesus our Lord.

ROMANS 8:38-39

GOOD SOIL
REQUIRES
A MIX OF
LIFE AND
DEATH.

Rocks

rock

[ˈräk] NOUN
1. a concreted mass
of stony material

also : broken pieces
of such masses

*R*ocks aren't simply obstacles the vinedresser has to contend with; they're something grapes *require* in order to thrive.

If the grape plant's sunshiny field isn't rocky enough, she'll be all showy, with lush green leaves, but bear little fruit. If the grape plant's field is too rocky, she'll lack enough earth for hearty roots and mournfully shrivel up. Thus, the landowner looking for the perfect place to plant his choice vine looks for a great spot in a decent climate with generous access to sun, an aspect that can soak in water but also drain it, and the right amount of rocks to make things just challenging enough for his vines to be a little uncomfortable.

Count it all joy, my brothers, when you meet trials of various kinds,

for you know that the testing of your faith produces steadfastness.

And let steadfastness have its full effect, that you may be

perfect and complete, lacking in nothing.

JAMES 1:2-4

BEARING FRUIT
IS POSSIBLE ONLY
WHEN WE'RE A LITTLE
UNCOMFORTABLE.

Hypaethral

hy·pae·thral

[hī-ˈpē-thrəl]

ADJECTIVE

1. having a roofless
central space

Hypaethral basically means roofless. Certain brands of miracles are reserved for open cathedrals. They only happen *out there* in the elements.

Out there, we find ourselves under the stars that God calls by name, and we are made small against the expanse of the heavens.

Out there, we discover that we are all uninsulated and vulnerable.

Out there, floodwaters rise and winds beat relentlessly against us. Out there, we plant seeds and then stare for days at the bare ground, wondering if anything at all will sprout and if a few dry days are signs of drought. Out there, we can't always tell the wheat from the tares. Out there, we can feel our hunger and thirst for something real, something whole—something that gets numbed indoors by cream soda and cheese puffs.

Out there, we have an unobstructed view of the horizon, where we can spot the silhouettes of prodigals coming home. Out there, we can smell the sheep before we can see them. We can feel the sunshine after a cold, dark night. Out there, we discover treasures that are hidden in a field rather than in a safe deposit box. Out there, we see crosses being dragged through the dirt instead of hanging in sanctuaries.

When I look at the night sky and see the work of your fingers—

the moon and the stars you set in place—

what are mere mortals that you should think about them,

human beings that you should care for them?

Yet you made them only a little lower than God

and crowned them with glory and honor.

PSALM 8:3-5, NLT

CERTAIN BRANDS
OF MIRACLES
ONLY HAPPEN
OUTDOORS.

Inspection

in·spec·tion
_____

[in-ˈspek-shən] NOUN
1. the act of viewing closely
in critical appraisal

*O*nly one thing is worse than producing no fruit: producing bad fruit. What's confusing to a world full of amateur fruit inspectors is how similar a bitter grape can look to a sweet one.

Since the Father calls Jesus-followers to live immensely fruitful lives, it stands to reason that no question is more relevant than this: What kind of fruit are we producing?

We can't see fruit the way God can, but with His help, we are fully capable of distinguishing between good fruit and bad fruit.

Inspection becomes an act of obedience. Keep in mind, we're not just on the hunt for bad fruit. We're also on the lookout for good fruit. If we think we have a God who only convicts and never encourages, who only tells us what's wrong with us and never what's right, we've probably created a god made in the image of a human authority who scarred us. We're safe and loved by God, no matter what kind of fruit we're currently producing.

What's the best way to tell what kind of fruit is being produced in your life? Look for evidence of the fruit of the Spirit—things like "love, joy, peace, patience, kindness, goodness, faithfulness, gentleness, [and] self-control" (Galatians 5:22-23). If the action or approach is quenching qualities of the Spirit, it's producing bad fruit. If it's evidencing qualities of the Spirit, it's producing good fruit.

The fruit of the Spirit is

love, joy, peace, forbearance,

kindness, goodness, faithfulness,

gentleness and self-control.

Against such things there is no law.

GALATIANS 5:22-23, NIV

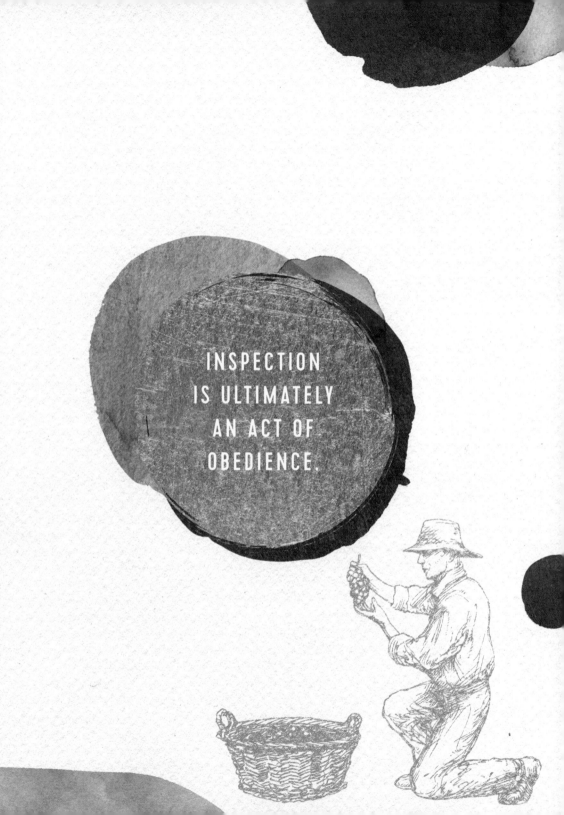

INSPECTION
IS ULTIMATELY
AN ACT OF
OBEDIENCE.

Branches

branch

['branch] NOUN
1. a natural subdivision
of a plant stem

*T*he job of the branch is to abide. Fruit is assured to every branch that fulfills its singular task: abide in the Vine. "Easy," we say, and we then spend a lifetime relapsing into autonomy and then repenting, relearning what it means to abide.

In one sense, abiding sounds like the easiest command for a Jesus-follower to undertake. It means resting in the One who is stronger than we are, wiser than we are, and more powerful than we are—and who loves us and defends us. But for most of us, the not-doing is infinitely more difficult than the doing. Give us a to-do list or a deadline or an assignment, but for the love, please don't ask us to let go and be still.

This is a good time to nail down an important principle of abiding. Abiding doesn't mean you're immobilized. That's the beauty of Christ turning this metaphor on its head. The vine, which was once the land, has now been supplanted by Christ. That means we no longer abide in a place but in a person. We reside in Jesus. When He moves, we move. When He stays, we stay.

And as counterintuitive as it may seem, walking and abiding are not antithetical.

By this we may know that we are in him:

whoever says he abides in him ought to walk

in the same way in which he walked.

1 JOHN 2:5-6

WE NO LONGER
ABIDE IN A PLACE.
WE NOW ABIDE
IN A PERSON.

Pruning

prune

[ˈprün] VERB
1. to cut off or cut back
parts of for better shape
or more fruitful growth

$\mathcal{N}$othing is more painful to the branch than pruning—and nothing is more irresponsible for the vinedresser than avoiding it.

For some of us, the pruning begins early in life; others may remain relatively intact until the later decades of life. By no means is all loss pruning, but pruning can certainly look like loss.

And yet God is never closer to us than He is during the pruning process. He can't avoid holding a branch when He's pinching off blooms with His thumbnail. With God as Gardener, pruning is always a hands-on endeavor. He can't let us go when He's cutting us back. His tending is never impersonal. Never mechanical. If we allow the shears to do their work, the purpose is always the same: growth.

Pruning, according to Jesus, is a really good sign. It doesn't just signal future fruit. It's proof of previous fruit.

Every branch in me that does not bear fruit he takes away,

and every branch that does bear fruit he prunes, that it may

bear more fruit.

JOHN 15:2

PRUNING HURTS.
BUT IT'S
PROOF OF FRUIT.

Transplant

trans·plant

[tran(t)s-ˈplant] VERB
1. to remove from one place
and settle or introduce
elsewhere; relocate

Nothing can get more confusing than feeling planted somewhere you're sure is home and then getting uprooted and transplanted somewhere else. Without warning, you face the prospect of having to start all over again. You had your sense of place. You thought you knew how this was going to go. Your future seemed clear. Your people were near. And now you feel like a stranger in a foreign land.

Sometimes you'll stay in that unfamiliar land for longer than you ever imagined. Other times God will pluck you up and move you right back to your homeland, only for you to come to the bewildering reality that, although the place hasn't changed, you have.

Nothing haunts us more than our search for, finally, a sense of place. As it turns out, true belonging is found only in the sovereign palm of God. There alone we find our place, even amid the seasons of moving, planting, uprooting, and replanting.

It's only when we find our place in Him that we find rest.

Though the path to this discovery is often painful, the discovery itself can be a relief—and not only to us. It gives us space to spread out and grow, and it relieves our other loves of a burden too big to carry.

And there we can bear mysterious fruit.

Let all that I am wait quietly before God,

    for my hope is in him.

He alone is my rock and my salvation,

    my fortress where I will not be shaken.

My victory and honor come from God alone.

    He is my refuge, a rock where no enemy can reach me.

O my people, trust in him at all times.

    Pour out your heart to him,

    for God is our refuge.

PSALM 62:5-8, NLT

WE LIVE
OUR LIVES
LOOKING
FOR HOME.

Overcropping

o·ver·crop

[ˈō-vər-ˈkräp] VERB
1. to exhaust the
fertility of by excessive
production without the
application of adequate
fertilizer to the soil

*W*e dwell in an age of aesthetics, where beauty is chief among aims. The purpose of the branch, however, is not the beauty of a painter's canvas—a well-tended vine covered in leaves misty with dew, filtered through the light of dawn.

The vinedresser doesn't bother pruning branches that don't bear fruit. He prunes those that do. Otherwise the vines will experience suffocation by overcrowding, or what the experts call "overcropping."

Receiving a cutback for impressive production is counterintuitive to us mortals, particularly in a screen-driven world where the bigger the bytes, the better the product. God, however, doesn't appear to mind being misunderstood. His determination to do us good is undeterred by accusations that He's doing us harm.

He controls the metaphor; the metaphor does not control Him. That means He can get creative with His shears. But I'll tell you what God can't do: He can't do evil. He can't be unloving, because He Himself is love. His goodness is inseparable from His glory (Exodus 33:18-19). So you can believe, as David did, that you will see the goodness of the Lord in the land of the living (Psalm 27:13).

"Come, let us go up to the mountain of the LORD,

   to the house of the God of Jacob,

that he may teach us his ways

   and that we may walk in his paths."

For out of Zion shall go forth the law,

   and the word of the LORD from Jerusalem.

He shall judge between the nations,

   and shall decide disputes for many peoples;

and they shall beat their swords into plowshares,

   and their spears into pruning hooks;

nation shall not lift up sword against nation,

   neither shall they learn war anymore.

ISAIAH 2:3-4

IN THE END,
PRUNING
IS A PAINFUL
MERCY.

Fertilization

fer·til·i·za·tion

[ˌfər-tə-lə-ˈzā-shən] NOUN
1. an act adding a substance
(such as manure or a chemical
mixture) to make soil more
productive

*L*et there be no mistaking that people of God, the chosen branches of the perfect Vine, can bear unripe, sour, bitter, rotten, and foul-smelling fruit. I've done it. I've also seen it, smelled it, and eaten it. We can even be moral and religiously upright and produce rotten fruit.

Molded, marred, or bug-scarred fruit is no welcome sight. But we will always be better off knowing. Delusion never delivers. Denial can't sweeten acrid grapes. But hard work now can produce a different crop next year.

The vinedresser does a curious thing with the rotten fruit. He turns it back into the soil and there, underground, by some spectacular organic miracle of nature, it fertilizes a future harvest.

Remember not the former things,

nor consider the things of old.

Behold, I am doing a new thing;

now it springs forth, do you not perceive it?

I will make a way in the wilderness

and rivers in the desert.

ISAIAH 43:18-19

REMEMBER NOT
THE FORMER
THINGS . . .

Trellis

trel·lis

[ˈtre-ləs] NOUN

1. a frame of latticework
used as a screen or as a
support for climbing plants

*T*he trellis offers the vinedresser the structure to spread out the grape canopy and keep it untangled as it grows. Without it, parts of the plant would be bullied into the shadows by more aggressive branches. These weaker branches would then be starved of the sunlight and circulation they need to thrive.

Without a trellis, the vine would fold in on itself, remaining stuck at ground level. Without a trellis, the branches would never reach their heads up to the sun.

And so the trellis of the Cross trains us in the way of forgiveness (Luke 23:33-35). It lifts our heads from the dirt and sludge and raises our faces to the Son.

Since God chose you to be the holy people he loves,

you must clothe yourselves with tenderhearted mercy,

kindness, humility, gentleness, and patience.

Make allowance for each other's faults,

and forgive anyone who offends you.

Remember, the Lord forgave you,

so you must forgive others.

COLOSSIANS 3:12-13, NLT

LIFT
YOUR HEAD,
AND TURN
YOUR FACE
TO THE SON.

Training

train

['trān] VERB
1. to direct the growth
of (a plant) usually by
bending, pruning, and
tying

*T*he vinedresser establishes a training system for his vine, or he is no vinedresser at all. When the trunk of a vine reaches around twelve inches tall, the vinedresser ties it to some form of stake. If he fails to do so, all hopes of a quality harvest are vanquished. With every three or four inches of growth comes another tie.

Stroll through the rows of any functioning vineyard, and you'll notice that the posture of a grapevine is a direct reflection of the apparatus it's attached to. Simply put, the way it's trained is the way it will grow. The apparatus may be anything from a single grape stake to an elaborate archway trellis, but whatever form it takes, the growing vine needs adequate support. The branches cannot carry the weight of immense fruitfulness on their own.

The Cross of Christ is our training. When the branch abides in the Vine, forgiveness is wholly unobstructed. It flows freely, both vertically and horizontally.

Welcome, one and all, to the way of the Cross.

The grace of God has appeared, bringing salvation for all people, training us to renounce ungodliness and worldly passions, and to live self-controlled, upright, and godly lives in the present age, waiting for our blessed hope, the appearing of the glory of our great God and Savior Jesus Christ, who gave himself for us to redeem us from all lawlessness and to purify for himself a people for his own possession who are zealous for good works.

TITUS 2:11-14

THE WAY
WE'RE TRAINED
IS THE WAY
WE GROW.

Fertile

fer·tile

['fər-t³l] ADJECTIVE
1. producing or bearing
many crops in great
quantities; productive

*T*he fertile hill Isaiah spoke of (Isaiah 5:1) could have been the most spectacular spot on earth, with perfect aspect and magnificent aesthetics. It could have been hemmed in by a wall of gleaming limestone and guarded from a grand limestone tower, with no expense spared. But if its soil hadn't been fertile, all would have been futile.

Merriam-Webster's definition of the word *fertile* is as far as we'd have to look for proof of a connection between fertile ground and fruit bearing. The first definition sounds like it could be describing the hillsides of Tuscany: "producing or bearing fruit in great quantities; productive."

So what makes soil fertile and therefore good?

The answer may surprise you. Good soil is a curious and compelling combination of life and death. So vital is death to the soil that life cannot exist there without it. The decaying matter from animals and plants is an essential source of nutrients in sustaining life.

Take a teaspoon from your kitchen drawer and dig up one spoonful of healthy soil, and you'll hold in your steady hand multimillions of microorganisms in one of the most impressive combinations of living matter known to humankind.

The point is, some variety of dying always precedes resurrection living. That's how salvation goes, but it's also how the saved grow. God knows that the most fertile soil for growing anything of value, certainly anything that bears fruit, is a well-blended, purposeful mass of life and death, of germination and decay.

Unless a grain of wheat falls into the earth and dies,

it remains alone; but if it dies, it bears much fruit.

JOHN 12:24

SOME MANNER
OF DYING
ALWAYS PRECEDES
RESURRECTION
LIVING.

Stakes

stake

['stāk] NOUN
1. a pointed piece of wood
or other material driven
or to be driven into the
ground as a marker or
support

The Cross of Christ is our stake in the ground. It is immovable. It is nonnegotiable. Let others be tied to whatever they please, but we are tied to the Cross. There is no playing it down. There is no dressing it up. There is no gospel without it.

The Cross remains our only means of finding true life—not just after we shed these temporal bodies, but right here, right now. On this very earth, in this very era, on the very block where we live.

When they came to a place called The Skull, they
nailed him to the cross. And the criminals were
also crucified—one on his right and one on his left.

Jesus said, "Father, forgive them, for they don't
know what they are doing." And the soldiers
gambled for his clothes by throwing dice.

The crowd watched and the leaders scoffed.
"He saved others," they said, "let him save himself
if he is really God's Messiah, the Chosen One."

LUKE 23:33-35, NLT

THE CROSS
IS OUR STAKE
IN THE GROUND.

Fruitfulness

fruit·ful·ness

[ˈfrüt-fəl-nəs] NOUN
1. yielding or producing
fruit; conducive to an
abundant yield

*W*e were created to contribute, fashioned to bring who we are and what we have to the human mix to add some measure of benefit. This was true even in Eden's unmarred paradise. God said to Adam and Eve, in so many words, "Add to it! Work the ground! And the two of you, be fruitful and multiply. Fill the earth!"

Jesus elevated the concept to another stratosphere by taking individuals He'd given abundant life to and, by the power of His own Spirit, making their contributions matter not just temporally, as He did with Adam and Eve, but eternally.

And it's not just us—God wants our lives to matter too. He means for us to be profoundly effective. That longing in us to contribute, to do something worthwhile, isn't just a self-consumed dream. If we follow Jesus, that's what we can hope to expect from life.

And being fruitful isn't some stale and banal duty. It directly affects how happy we are, because engaging in what God is doing is the only thing that gives us true satisfaction and peace. God is invading the globe with the gospel of Christ, pursuing people from every tongue, tribe, and nation, offering them life, faith, love, hope, deliverance, joy, and a forever future where He reigns as King.

Nothing happening on earth is more meaningful or exhilarating. And as we bear much fruit, we get to be part of it.

By this my Father is glorified,

that you bear much fruit

and so prove to be my disciples. . . .

You did not choose me, but I chose you

and appointed you that you should go

and bear fruit and

that your fruit should abide.

JOHN 15:8, 16

152

GOD IS
INVADING THE GLOBE
WITH HIS LOVE.
AND YOU GET TO BE
PART OF IT.

Reproduction

155

re·pro·duc·tion

[ˌrē-prə-ˈdək-shən] NOUN
1. the act of producing new
individuals of the same
kind again

*G*ive the grapevine a favorable environment and it will choose to take the vegetative route: that is, it will put its energies into making leaves and shoots.

Effectively, it is saying, "This is a fine spot, I'm going to make myself at home here." It won't be too bothered about making grapes. But make things difficult for the vine, by restricting water supply, making nutrients scarce, pruning it hard and crowding it with close neighbors, and it will take the hump.

It will sense that this is not the ideal place to be a grapevine. Instead of devoting itself to growing big and sprawling, it will focus its effort on reproducing itself, which for a vine means making grapes.

As long as the grape plant is feeling comfortable and unchallenged, she will gleefully leaf. She will award leaves, leaves, and leaves upon leaves to her sweet-natured host. She will bear wreaths of leaves to her happy heart's content. Eventually she will become so thick with leaves that the hungry passerby will observe, "There's nary a cluster to eat."

The grape plant reproduces when she gets concerned that her survival is at risk. She responds to the threat by doing her best to ensure that her kind makes it even if she doesn't.

Abide in me, and I in you. As the branch cannot

bear fruit by itself, unless it abides in the vine,

neither can you, unless you abide in me.

JOHN 15:4

HEAVEN FORBID
THAT WE SHOULD
BE ALL LEAVES
AND NO FRUIT.

Cultivation

cul·ti·va·tion
———
[ˌkəl-tə-ˈvā-shən] NOUN
1. the act of preparing for
the raising of crops

*T*he Man of Sorrows was simultaneously the Man of Joys—in ways perhaps beyond our comprehension but not entirely beyond our experience. As we try to grow a vineyard from ground to ripe grape in the soil of our imagination, we may recognize many of the hardships and challenges of preparing a vineyard. But I have a hunch we often underestimate just how joyful cultivation can be.

After all the laboring, rock clearing, hoeing, weeding, waiting, growing, staking, guarding, pruning, weather watching, and clock watching, the time finally comes for grape picking. And as it turns out, with grape picking comes partying. I don't just mean there's a party at the end of the picking, although that's true, and it will hit fever pitch at that point. I mean there's partying in the midst of the picking.

Partying was God's idea in the first place. He strung festivals like holiday lights into the annual Hebrew calendar—seven in number, each commemorating His faithfulness, and He commanded His people to celebrate them.

God intended joy to be such an integral part of the harvest that, if it was missing, the people of God would know something was awry.

These things I have spoken to you,

that my joy may be in you,

and that your joy may be full.

JOHN 15:11

JOY
IS INTEGRAL TO
THE HARVEST.

Flourishing

flour·ish

['flər-ish] VERB

1. to grow luxuriantly;
thrive

*I*n the Old Testament, God's chosen people were the vine. Then Jesus arrived on the scene with this startling revelation: He Himself is the vine. And it gets better: He invites us to be connected to Him, to be rooted in Him, to abide with Him. There's nothing sweeter in life.

If you're in Christ, He is your true Vine, whether you realize it or not. But a whole new way of flourishing begins when you know it. When you count on it. When you live like it. When you let go of the vines you thought were giving you life.

He wants you to flourish in Him. Every last thing He plants in your life is intended for that purpose. If we give ourselves fully to His faithful ways, mysterious and painful though they may be at times, we will find that it's all part of the process that enables us to grow and bear fruit.

You brought a vine out of Egypt;

you drove out the nations and planted it.

You cleared the ground for it;

it took deep root and filled the land.

PSALM 80:8-9

GOD DOESN'T
WASTE A THING.
NOT A SINGLE THING.

Compost

com·post

[ˈkäm-ˌpōst] NOUN
1. a mixture that consists
largely of decayed
organic matter and is
used for fertilizing and
conditioning land

*N*obody told me a remotely productive life would involve quite so much manure. That's why I'm telling you. If you want to live an immensely fruitful life, you will have to deal with substantial piles of it. I wish I could tell you otherwise, but we both know better.

Don't get me wrong. I'm not saying you have to like the manure. But what you can come to appreciate is that the Vinedresser can use it as potent fertilizer toward some fine fruit in your life.

At first, the manure that gets heaped on you will appear to have no value at all. You won't seem to learn a thing from it except perhaps that people can be cruel. You'll go through an ordeal or an attack, an assessment or a critique that even years later you will think had no constructive element whatsoever. It just seems meaningless. But it's not.

God uses it—all of it. In the hands of the Vinedresser, nothing is dropped. Everything matters.

I want to know Christ and experience the mighty power

that raised him from the dead. I want to suffer with him,

sharing in his death, so that one way or another

I will experience the resurrection from the dead!

PHILIPPIANS 3:10-11, NLT

THE VINEDRESSER CAN USE THE CHALLENGES IN OUR LIVES AS POTENT FERTILIZER.

Gleaning

glean

[ˈglēn] VERB

1. to gather grain or other
produce left by reapers

The Lord gave specific instructions to His people about what to do with the gleanings after the harvest: "When you reap the harvest of your land, you shall not reap your field right up to its edge, nor shall you gather the gleanings after your harvest. You shall leave them for the poor and for the sojourner: I am the LORD your God" (Leviticus 23:22).

In essence, the Lord was saying, "Remember where you've been. Remember the rock from which you've been hewn. Remember that I redeemed you. You didn't do this for yourself. You have been the wanderer. You have been the dependent, cast upon on the mercy of strangers who owed you nothing. In your privilege, don't dare to overlook those without it."

Take a look at the edges of our fields, and you'll see people our society claims don't matter. But in God's eyes, every soul is of inestimable worth. And these people at the edges of the field are hungry. Hungry for love. Hungry for affection. Hungry for friendship. Hungry for a listening ear. Hungry for hope. Hungry to know God is there and that He cares. And I wonder—have we harvested with the margins in mind? Do we intentionally serve people on the edge?

We have gleaned such grace from the Vinedresser's field. Now it's our turn to give it.

Freely you have received; freely give.

MATTHEW 10:8, NIV

ONLY GOD CAN
SAVE THE WORLD.
BUT WE CAN
SERVE IT A
FRUIT PLATE.

Hardiness

har·di·ness

[ˈhär-dē-nəs] NOUN
1. the capability to
withstand adverse
conditions

I have a hunch that when it comes down to it, you're pretty tough . . . as long as the hard parts have a purpose. The Vinedresser understands that longing for meaning—in fact, He wired you that way. He puts down your roots in the kind of humus that will bring forth the most delectable grapes.

One of these days, when we get to talk with Jesus face-to-face and recount to Him how the pestilence nearly destroyed us, He might tell us, perhaps with a smile, that our souls were never at risk—and, really, neither was our fruitfulness. He never took His eyes off of us. He fought for us. He defended us. He took the assaults against us personally.

He never left us on that battlefield alone. He did for us what God did for Joseph in Genesis 49:24. When the demonic archers came for us, shooting bitter arrows, He caused our bow to remain steady, and our "arms were made agile by the hands of the Mighty One of Jacob."

Jesus knew how things would play out. He knew what we had in us when the devil came after us. He put it there Himself.

That's why you were allowed to be tested almost beyond what you could bear. He knew you'd prove genuine. Even when we fear we are fakes, Jesus knows better.[6]

He who dwells in the shelter of the Most High

will abide in the shadow of the Almighty.

I will say to the Lord, "My refuge and my fortress,

my God, in whom I trust."

For he will deliver you from the snare of the fowler

and from the deadly pestilence.

PSALM 91:1-3

GOD DOESN'T
CAUSE PESTILENCE.
BUT HE CERTAINLY
WON'T WASTE IT
EITHER.

Seasons

sea·son

[ˈsē-zᵊn] NOUN
1. a time characterized by a
particular circumstance or
feature; a period associated
with some phase or activity
of agriculture (such as
growth or harvesting)

*W*hen we're going through a difficult season, wouldn't the best news of all be that life would simply go back to normal someday? When the framework of our daily existence gets completely dismantled and the landscape around us grows increasingly unrecognizable, our strongest longing is seldom prosperity. What we yearn for is normalcy. We don't tend to ask for the moon when we've lost all we've known. We just want some semblance of our old lives back.

The hard truth is, there's no real going back. But once we get up again, there can be a going forward. In His faithfulness, God sees to it what we thought was the end isn't the end after all.

If we can't have our treasured yesterday back, at least tomorrow can matter. The wonder of fruit bearing is that something meaningful can come from the meanest of seasons. What we endured matters.

For everything there is a season, and a time for every matter under heaven:

a time to be born, and a time to die;

a time to plant, and a time to pluck up what is planted;

a time to kill, and a time to heal;

a time to break down, and a time to build up;

a time to weep, and a time to laugh;

a time to mourn, and a time to dance;

a time to cast away stones, and a time to gather stones together;

a time to embrace, and a time to refrain from embracing;

a time to seek, and a time to lose;

a time to keep, and a time to cast away;

a time to tear, and a time to sew;

a time to keep silence, and a time to speak;

a time to love, and a time to hate;

a time for war, and a time for peace.

ECCLESIASTES 3:1-8

MEANING
CAN COME IN
THE MEANEST
OF SEASONS.

Dormancy

dor·man·cy

[ˈdȯr-mən(t)-sē] NOUN
1. marked by a suspension
of biological activity;
the state of not actively
growing but being
protected from the
environment

*I*t happens in every life: unwanted changes occur. Crises happen. Catastrophes invade our days without warning. The enemy comes to steal, kill, and destroy. He wages threats and makes good on some of them. From all appearances, the pleasant field that once surrounded us—increasingly pleasant, in retrospect—has been scorched and razed. However, God makes threats of His own, and He never wastes His breath. Whether or not our physical surroundings ever again resemble what we once knew, if we have an ounce of breath on the other side, we can bear much fruit again.

Maybe right now that promise doesn't mean a lot. You don't want a remnant; you want all the same people back. And truth be told, you'd prefer them at all their former ages and stages. You don't want to grow something new. You want to return to your old life. You want those exact clusters of grapes, not new ones. You want everything to taste exactly like it once did. I understand. But in time, finding fruitfulness again will make more difference than you can imagine.

The branch is very much alive and never more poised for fruitfulness than in the wake of winter.

The one who sows to his own flesh

will from the flesh reap corruption,

but the one who sows to the Spirit

will from the Spirit reap eternal life.

And let us not grow weary of doing good,

for in due season we will reap, if we do not give up.

GALATIANS 6:8-9

DORMANT
DOES NOT MEAN
DEAD.

Cultivar

cul·ti·var

[ˈkəl-tə-ˌvär] NOUN
1. an organism,
especially one of
an agricultural or
horticultural variety,
originating under
cultivation (from
*culti*vated + *var*iety)

We are each called, male and female alike, to be part of the Vine's cultivar, or purposefully cultivated variety. From the very start, Jesus called both men and women to His gospel work. God poured out His spirit on His sons and His daughters, and He wastes no willing life.

In the Gospels, Jesus depicts a kind of fruit-bearing that the Father prizes above all others. Every life that's attached to Him possesses the supernatural capacity to be stupendously productive. Like the natural grape plant, however, we might be inclined to wonder sometimes whether the ground where we're planted is trying to cultivate us or kill us.

Welcome to the fruitful vineyard, where grapes grow only in tension.

In those days I will pour out my Spirit

even on my servants—men and women alike—

and they will prophesy.

ACTS 2:18, NLT

GROWTH
ONLY HAPPENS
IN TENSION.

Ripe

ripe

[ˈrīp] ADJECTIVE
1. fully grown and
developed; mature

*W*hen you arrive in heaven, I imagine Jesus will meet you at the gates, throw His arms around you, and then give you a retrospective tour of your life.

Jesus will point and say, "See that rocky patch over there? The rough terrain that tore the soles from your shoes and left your feet black and blue? It was part of making you into the person you are now."

You'll see a place you lived for a spell, a place you never would have chosen if it had been up to you. "That spot was no accident," He'll say. "You were right where you were supposed to be. In fact, that was sacred ground."

Then He'll take you back to the most excruciating scenes you endured. The place where you were pruned within an inch of your life. The place where pestilence nearly finished you off. But this time you won't see the pruning shears or the blight-eaten leaves.

You'll see only the beauty that came from ashes, the joy that sprung out of mourning, the praise that grew out of the soil of despair.

Finally Jesus will show you a field with basket upon basket of plump ripe grapes. "Where did this harvest come from?" you'll wonder.

The Vinedresser will grin from ear to ear. "This is the fruit of your life. You know how I like to make things grow."

Then He'll put His arm around you. "There was never a moment I wasn't with you. I was singing over you the whole time."

He has sent me to tell those who mourn

that the time of the LORD's favor has come. . . .

To all who mourn in Israel,

he will give a crown of beauty for ashes,

a joyous blessing instead of mourning,

festive praise instead of despair. . . .

Instead of shame and dishonor,

you will enjoy a double share of honor.

You will possess a double portion of prosperity in your land,

and everlasting joy will be yours. . . .

The Sovereign LORD will show his justice to the nations of the world.

Everyone will praise him!

His righteousness will be like a garden in early spring,

with plants springing up everywhere.

ISAIAH 61:2-3, 7, 11, NLT

THERE HAS
NEVER BEEN
A MOMENT
HE WASN'T
WITH YOU.

Harvest

har·vest

['här-vəst] NOUN
1. a mature crop (as of
grain or fruit); yield

The promise of fruit from the vine and the tree isn't just about food. It is about hope. It offers thriving evidence of a destiny fulfilled. It means that the land, the grape plant, and the fig tree are doing what they were created to do: produce fruit.

Hope doesn't happen in a vacuum. There's a hidden knowing inherent in hope. In order to exist and persist, hope knows something real, however faint it may seem. That knowing is what we call faith. And faith is not wispy. It's no wishing upon a star. It is a white-knuckle conviction of what we cannot see.

We know a better world is coming, though we don't know when and even the best theologians can't explain exactly how. We know an eternal God won't stop until He has brought everything full circle. We know because He said so. As surely as God redeemed humans from the curse of sin through the Cross, He will redeem the earth from the curse of sin that caused the ground to rebel against the work of human hands.

He who supplies seed to the sower and

bread for food will supply and multiply your

seed for sowing and increase the harvest of your righteousness.

You will be enriched in every way to be generous in every way,

which through us will produce thanksgiving to God.

2 CORINTHIANS 9:10-11

YOU WILL
REAP A HARVEST
OF HOPE.

Viticulture

vi·ti·cul·ture

[ˈvi-tə-ˌkəl-chər] NOUN
1. the cultivation or culture
of grapes especially for
wine making

There are some mysteries in viticulture that can't be fully satisfied scientifically. They are simply meant to be appreciated. The finest vinedressers in Tuscany could plant a vine in a perfect spot, but they can't make the soil comply. They could choose the right climate, but they can't control the weather. They could strive for consistency in water and fertilizer, but they can't force the vine to produce the same wine produced by its neighbor tied to the next trellis. The mysteries of viticulture can be studied, but they can't all be solved.

It's not so different from the life of faith. As much as we'd like a formula to guarantee how our lives will turn out, we find ourselves long on mystery and short on control. Instead of a formula, God gives us an invitation, a relationship. We can't control Him; we always predict Him. But one thing we can do: trust Him. And then lean into the mystery.

Farmers who wait for perfect weather never plant.

If they watch every cloud, they never harvest.

Just as you cannot understand the path of the wind or

the mystery of a tiny baby growing in its mother's womb,

so you cannot understand the activity of God,

who does all things.

ECCLESIASTES 11:4-5, NLT

THERE ARE
SOME MYSTERIES
THAT CAN'T BE
FULLY SATISFIED
BY REASON
AND LOGIC.

Vintage

vin·tage

['vin-tij] NOUN

1. a season's yield
of grapes from a
vineyard

*W*hen the conditions are right, a single vine can produce around three thousand grapes. All that growing isn't just for you; God designed you to produce a harvest that will long outlast your life. And when your vintage on earth comes to an end, He invites you to the ultimate feast . . . at His own table.

When that day comes, we will attend a wedding feast to exceed all wedding feasts—even the famous one in Cana. We will rejoice and exult. And after all our self-awareness and self-consciousness, don't tell me that exulting won't be refreshing.

We're going to be happier than we can imagine.

On this mountain the LORD Almighty will prepare

a feast of rich food for all peoples,

a banquet of aged wine—

the best of meats and the finest of wines.

ISAIAH 25:6, NIV

YOUR
HARVEST
CAN LONG
OUTLAST
YOUR LIFE.

NOTES

1. Walter William Skeat, *A Concise Etymological Dictionary of the English Language* (London: Clarendon Press, 1885), 211.

2. L. H. Bailey in Jeff Cox, *From Vines to Wines: The Complete Guide to Growing Grapes and Making Your Own Wine* (North Adams, MA: Storey, 2015), 14.

3. Robert E. White, *Understanding Vineyard Soils* (Oxford: Oxford University Press, 2009), 25.

4. White, 17.

5. White, 175.

6. Parts of this passage originally appeared in Beth Moore, "To Servants of Jesus in Your 30s and 40s," *The LMP Blog*, May 23, 2016, https://blog.lproof.org/2016/05/to-servants-of-jesus-in-your-30s-and-40s.html.

ART CREDITS

About the Author

Author and speaker Beth Moore is a dynamic teacher whose conferences take her across the globe. She has written numerous bestselling books and Bible studies, including *Chasing Vines*; *So Long, Insecurity*; *Breaking Free*; *Believing God*; *Entrusted*; and *The Quest*, which have been read by women of all ages, races, and denominations. Another recent addition includes her first work of fiction, *The Undoing of Saint Silvanus*. Beth recently celebrated twenty years of Living Proof Live conferences. She can be seen teaching Bible studies on the television program *Living Proof with Beth Moore*, aired on the Trinity Broadcasting Network.

JOIN BETH ON HER JOURNEY OF DISCOVERING
WHAT IT MEANS TO CHASE VINES—AND LEARN HOW
TO FULLY EMBRACE GOD'S AMAZING DESIGN FOR A
fruitful, abundant, and meaningful life.

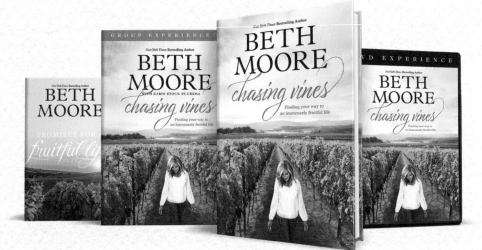

Popular teacher and speaker *Beth Moore* helps us understand how our life—and our relationship with God—can be different if we better grasp His amazing design for making lives that matter. Through the *Chasing Vines* suite of products, explore the ways God delights in watching things grow—and how the land of the vineyard holds the secret for how we can have a fruitful life.

To learn more from Beth and access additional resources, visit her online at www.bethmoore.org.

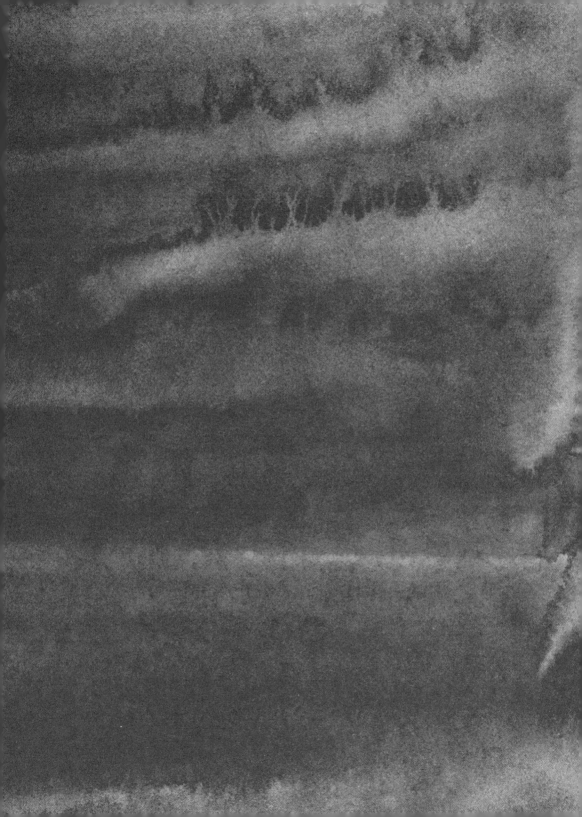